How To Be The Woman Of Your Husband's Dreams. . .and not his worst nightmare!

How To Be The Woman Of Your Husband's Dreams . . .
And Not His Worst Nightmare!
ISBN 0-88144-187-2
Copyright © 1995 by Trade Life
Tulsa, Oklahoma 74155

Introduction

How To Be The Woman Of Your Husband's Dreams . . . And Not His Worst Nightmare! is a delightfully amusing combination of truth and jest. Filled with quotes which alternately poke fun at and lend tremendous insight into everyday married life, this clever little pocketbook will bring a chuckle and perhaps a playful wince now and then to men and women alike.

These quotes will entertain couples who have been married for years, those recently engaged or married, and singles who ever entertained the thought! Overflowing with both wit and wisdom, *How To Be The Woman Of Your Husband's Dreams . . . And Not His Worst Nightmare!* will be perfect gift for Valentine's Day, your best friends' wedding showers and anniversaries, and all around special occasions.

This little pocketbook of quotes will encourage you to both laugh and learn! Be sure to put this humorous keepsake on your coffee table for interesting conversation and table talk, then give one to a friend to bring a ray of light-hearted sunshine into another life.

And don't forget to pick up a copy of its companion pocketbook, *How To Be The Man Of Your Wife's Dreams . . . And Not Her Worst Nightmare!* Then sit back, laugh, and have a jolly good time!

Surprise him Saturday night with a homemade dinner of 16-ounce sirloin, baked potato, caesar salad, and apple pie a' la mode.

HOW TO BE THE WOMAN OF YOUR HUSBAND'S DREAMS

Tell him to pull out last week's pizza from the freezer.

AND NOT HIS WORST NIGHTMARE

Convince him that you adore his body.

HOW TO BE THE WOMAN OF YOUR HUSBAND'S DREAMS

Slip a fat gram counter into his briefcase.

AND NOT HIS WORST NIGHTMARE

Work hard to make his home a castle.

HOW TO BE THE WOMAN OF YOUR HUSBAND'S DREAMS

Remind him that you hate living in a dump.

AND NOT HIS WORST NIGHTMARE

9

When you need his help, make a simple request.

HOW TO BE THE WOMAN OF YOUR HUSBAND'S DREAMS

Elicit his help by
yelling, "Move it!"

11

When he touches you, whisper that he is your *"sexy beast."*

12

HOW TO BE THE WOMAN OF YOUR HUSBAND'S DREAMS

Shout, "Get away from me, you animal!"

When he lets you know
he is feeling amorous,
whisper sweet
nothings in his ear.

14

HOW TO BE THE WOMAN OF YOUR HUSBAND'S DREAMS

Respond to his advances
by laughing hideously
and snarling:
"Get real!"

AND NOT HIS WORST NIGHTMARE

Saturday morning make breakfast and serve it to him in bed.

HOW TO BE THE WOMAN OF YOUR HUSBAND'S DREAMS

As soon as he opens his eyes, shove a list of chores in his face.

17

AND NOT HIS WORST NIGHTMARE

Before he comes to bed, turn back the covers and spray mist his favorite perfume across the sheets.

HOW TO BE THE WOMAN OF YOUR HUSBAND'S DREAMS

Hop into bed with your sweats on after you get back from your two-mile jog.

AND NOT HIS WORST NIGHTMARE

When he needs you most, just sit and listen.

HOW TO BE THE WOMAN OF YOUR HUSBAND'S DREAMS

When he needs you most, insist he "wait a minute!" while you finish sweeping the kitchen floor.

AND NOT HIS WORST NIGHTMARE

Straighten the house and get all dolled up to meet him at the door.

HOW TO BE THE WOMAN OF YOUR HUSBAND'S DREAMS

Meet him at the door in your terry cloth robe and curlers.

AND NOT HIS WORST NIGHTMARE

23

Surprise him with the new *Sports Illustrated*.

HOW TO BE THE WOMAN OF YOUR HUSBAND'S DREAMS

Leave the room and slam the door when he turns on the ball game.

AND NOT HIS WORST NIGHTMARE

25

Let him know how much you'd like to spend an entire week-end alone with him.

HOW TO BE THE WOMAN OF YOUR HUSBAND'S DREAMS

When he invites you to go away for the weekend, suggest spending time with your mother.

AND NOT HIS WORST NIGHTMARE

Leave him a steamy note on the mirror in the morning telling him you can't wait to see him that night.

HOW TO BE THE WOMAN OF YOUR HUSBAND'S DREAMS

Leave him a list on the mirror that morning detailing things he needs to do that day.

AND NOT HIS WORST NIGHTMARE

29

When he's talking
to you, hold him close
and rub his back.

HOW TO BE THE WOMAN OF YOUR HUSBAND'S DREAMS

When he's trying to talk to you, stare into the mirror and pluck your eyebrows.

AND NOT HIS WORST NIGHTMARE

Just before he comes home from work, shower and put on his favorite perfume.

HOW TO BE THE WOMAN OF YOUR HUSBAND'S DREAMS

Shower and brush your teeth every third day.

AND NOT HIS WORST NIGHTMARE

34

To soothe him at the end
of a long, stressful day,
rest his head in your lap
and softly stroke his face.

HOW TO BE THE WOMAN OF YOUR HUSBAND'S DREAMS

When he walks in the door late that night, meet him at the door with your two year old and tell him it's his turn.

AND NOT HIS WORST NIGHTMARE

36

Help him with the yard work.

After his long day in the yard, ask him why your yard doesn't look like the neighbor's.

AND NOT HIS WORST NIGHTMARE

Call him during the day; ask him if there is anything he needs for you to pick up while you're out shopping.

HOW TO BE THE WOMAN OF YOUR HUSBAND'S DREAMS

Whine into the phone that you need him to run an errand for you on his way home.

AND NOT HIS WORST NIGHTMARE.

39

First thing in the morning when he is just waking up, bring him a cup of coffee and a kiss.

HOW TO BE THE WOMAN OF YOUR HUSBAND'S DREAMS

Hold the alarm clock next to his ear; shake him two or three times; then holler, "It's morning! Get up and make the coffee!"

AND NOT HIS WORST NIGHTMARE

Buy him his favorite cologne.

HOW TO BE THE WOMAN OF YOUR HUSBAND'S DREAMS

Buy him deodorant.

Instead of buying
yourself a new outfit,
pick him up a new
set of tools.

44

Instead of buying
yourself a new outfit,
buy yourself two.

AND NOT HIS WORST NIGHTMARE

45

Turn on soft music and turn down the light.

HOW TO BE THE WOMAN OF YOUR HUSBAND'S DREAMS

Turn on Richard Simmons and tell him a little workout wouldn't hurt him.

AND NOT HIS WORST NIGHTMARE

Curl up close to him in bed.

HOW TO BE THE WOMAN OF YOUR HUSBAND'S DREAMS

Pick up a book and ignore him.

AND NOT HIS WORST NIGHTMARE

When he winks
at you in a crowd,
wink back.

HOW TO BE THE WOMAN OF YOUR HUSBAND'S DREAMS

Ask him where he got the twitch.

AND NOT HIS WORST NIGHTMARE

Put on romantic music and ask him to dance.

HOW TO BE THE WOMAN OF YOUR HUSBAND'S DREAMS

If he asks you to dance, say, "At home — alone?"

AND NOT HIS WORST NIGHTMARE

53

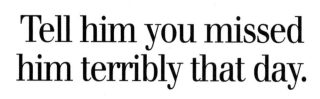

Tell him you missed him terribly that day.

HOW TO BE THE WOMAN OF YOUR HUSBAND'S DREAMS

When he comes home,
roll your eyes and
yell to the kids:
"Your father's home."

AND NOT HIS WORST NIGHTMARE

Reveal in a whisper
that your favorite person
in the world is him.

HOW TO BE THE WOMAN OF YOUR HUSBAND'S DREAMS

Go on and on about the
fine qualities of your
former boyfriend.

AND NOT HIS WORST NIGHTMARE

When you sense he
wants to be close,
surprise him and
be the aggressor.

HOW TO BE THE WOMAN OF YOUR HUSBAND'S DREAMS

Ignore him and
begin to balance
the checkbook.

AND NOT HIS WORST NIGHTMARE

Tell him he has a sexy grin.

HOW TO BE THE WOMAN OF YOUR HUSBAND'S DREAMS

Ask him when he's going to get his teeth fixed.

AND NOT HIS WORST NIGHTMARE

Make the first few minutes of his day *unforgettable*.

HOW TO BE THE WOMAN OF YOUR HUSBAND'S DREAMS

Make them something he'll want to *forget*!

AND NOT HIS WORST NIGHTMARE

Commend him
for his most recent
success at his new job.

HOW TO BE THE WOMAN OF YOUR HUSBAND'S DREAMS

Talk about the bucks your brother makes as an oil baron.

AND NOT HIS WORST NIGHTMARE

Run your fingers through his hair.

HOW TO BE THE WOMAN OF YOUR HUSBAND'S DREAMS

Ask where his hair went.

AND NOT HIS WORST NIGHTMARE

When he tells you
he is in the mood for
Surf and Turf, take him
to a fancy steakhouse.

68

HOW TO BE THE WOMAN OF YOUR HUSBAND'S DREAMS

Throw water in his face and hand him his running shoes.

AND NOT HIS WORST NIGHTMARE

69

For a birthday surprise, invite "the guys" over at 5 a.m. to pick him up for a full day of fishing or hunting.

HOW TO BE THE WOMAN OF YOUR HUSBAND'S DREAMS

Invite your family for the day.

AND NOT HIS WORST NIGHTMARE

Pray quietly for him regarding the concerns that are on his heart.

HOW TO BE THE WOMAN OF YOUR HUSBAND'S DREAMS

Notify him that he's either to shape up or ship out!

AND NOT HIS WORST NIGHTMARE

Invite him to sit outside with you to look at the moon and the stars.

HOW TO BE THE WOMAN OF YOUR HUSBAND'S DREAMS

When he has a free
evening, give yourself
a four-hour facial.

AND NOT HIS WORST NIGHTMARE

When he pines to have
a red Corvette one day, bring
him the brochures from the
car dealer to let him know
you support his dream.

HOW TO BE THE WOMAN OF YOUR HUSBAND'S DREAMS

Laugh and say:
"Yeah, right, after we
get my Jag, mink,
emerald ring. . . ."

AND NOT HIS WORST NIGHTMARE

Add zip to your
relationship!
Have a glamour photo
made of yourself in
a spellbinding dress.

HOW TO BE THE WOMAN OF YOUR HUSBAND'S DREAMS

Unzip your relationship
with a glamour photo
of yourself in a
spellbinding dress —
two sizes too small.

AND NOT HIS WORST NIGHTMARE

When he calls you on Wednesday to ask you for a date on Friday night, say with excitement, "I'd love to!"

HOW TO BE THE WOMAN OF YOUR HUSBAND'S DREAMS

When he bounces
in the door Friday night,
say, "I forgot."

AND NOT HIS WORST NIGHTMARE

Saturday morning, tell him that this is his day "off" and you've sent the kids to your mother's. Ask him to make a list of his favorite things and do them.

HOW TO BE THE WOMAN OF YOUR HUSBAND'S DREAMS

Sleep in till noon Saturday. Get up just long enough to tell him where the diapers are so he can change and feed the baby — and where the peanut butter is so he can fix the kids' lunch.

AND NOT HIS WORST NIGHTMARE

When he's sick, tuck him into bed and bring him homemade chicken soup; spoon feed him the first few bites.

HOW TO BE THE WOMAN OF YOUR HUSBAND'S DREAMS

Toss him the car keys; tell him to see the doctor and *not* to forget his medicine on the way home . . . like last time.

AND NOT HIS WORST NIGHTMARE

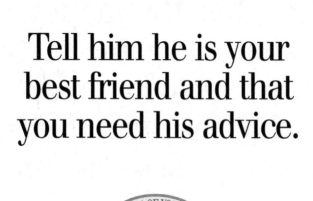

Tell him he is your best friend and that you need his advice.

HOW TO BE THE WOMAN OF YOUR HUSBAND'S DREAMS

86

When he tries to help you, listen intently, then do what you want.

AND NOT HIS WORST NIGHTMARE

Surprise him when
he comes in from work
with his favorite cold
drink, lighted candles,
and a hot bath.

HOW TO BE THE WOMAN OF YOUR HUSBAND'S DREAMS

Take your afternoon
nap each evening
from five to seven.

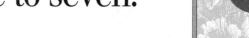

AND NOT HIS WORST NIGHTMARE

When he makes a
mistake, hug him
and tell him how
much you love him.

HOW TO BE THE WOMAN OF YOUR HUSBAND'S DREAMS

When he makes a
mistake, call the local
radio talk show.

AND NOT HIS WORST NIGHTMARE

While he cooks dinner for you, say, "Umm, what smells good?"

Sniff the air and say, "What's that smell?"

AND NOT HIS WORST NIGHTMARE

Shake up the routine!
Open the door for *him*
as he gets into the car.
Mow the lawn
while *he* relaxes.

HOW TO BE THE WOMAN OF YOUR HUSBAND'S DREAMS

When he shows signs of wanting to break out of the routine, get rigid!

AND NOT HIS WORST NIGHTMARE

Clean out that messy garage for him!

HOW TO BE THE WOMAN OF YOUR HUSBAND'S DREAMS

First chance you get,
point to the mess
in the garage.

AND NOT HIS WORST NIGHTMARE

When he hasn't
showered or shaved,
say, "You are so
good-looking!"

HOW TO BE THE WOMAN OF YOUR HUSBAND'S DREAMS

When he looks dreadful
and smells atrocious,
walk past him holding
your nose.

AND NOT HIS WORST NIGHTMARE

When he is apprehensive
about your finances, look
him in the eyes and
assure him you have
full confidence in him.

100

HOW TO BE THE WOMAN OF YOUR HUSBAND'S DREAMS

When he tells you he didn't get the raise, scream, "What did you do this time?!!"

AND NOT HIS WORST NIGHTMARE

When he tries to tell you that a habit of yours is bothering him, assure him you will work on it. Then do it.

HOW TO BE THE WOMAN OF YOUR HUSBAND'S DREAMS

Pick up another habit you know he hates.

AND NOT HIS WORST NIGHTMARE

103

If he urges you to become more of a recreational companion, join him the next time he wants to go fishing.

HOW TO BE THE WOMAN OF YOUR HUSBAND'S DREAMS

Tell him you get enough "recreation" picking up his clothes.

AND NOT HIS WORST NIGHTMARE

Call him at work just to tell him how much you miss him and can't wait to be with him.

HOW TO BE THE WOMAN OF YOUR HUSBAND'S DREAMS

When he calls you during the day, let the answering machine get it rather than let it disturb your nap.

AND NOT HIS WORST NIGHTMARE

A week before his birthday,
tell him you are planning
a special celebration just
for the two of you.
Then follow through.

108

Come up with some really convincing excuses why you didn't even get him a card, such as: "You always say not to make a fuss."

109

AND NOT HIS WORST NIGHTMARE

While driving long distances together, stop for a break and rub his neck and shoulders.

110

HOW TO BE THE WOMAN OF YOUR HUSBAND'S DREAMS

Talk for hours about every trivial matter you dealt with during the week, then tell him you're too tired to drive when it's your turn.

AND NOT HIS WORST NIGHTMARE

111

Spend a weekend
with him enjoying
only those activities and
foods that *he* likes best!

HOW TO BE THE WOMAN OF YOUR HUSBAND'S DREAMS

Spend a weekend
with your girlfriends.

AND NOT HIS WORST NIGHTMARE

Savor with him the taste of sweet, fresh cherries, grapes, pineapple, and strawberries. Feed them to him by hand.

HOW TO BE THE WOMAN OF YOUR HUSBAND'S DREAMS

Tell him if he'd eat raw vegetables he could take off that belly.

AND NOT HIS WORST NIGHTMARE

When he gains
a little weight,
overlook it.

HOW TO BE THE WOMAN OF YOUR HUSBAND'S DREAMS

Slip a picture of a hog into his briefcase.

AND NOT HIS WORST NIGHTMARE

On your twentieth anniversary, proclaim: "I am more attracted to you than I was twenty years ago."

HOW TO BE THE WOMAN OF YOUR HUSBAND'S DREAMS

Say to him, "My, how the years have *rolled* by. . .speaking of rolls, here's the 'Tummy Tamer' I got you."

AND NOT HIS WORST NIGHTMARE

120

Tell him you would love
to start contributing to
the charity of *his* choice.

HOW TO BE THE WOMAN OF YOUR HUSBAND'S DREAMS

Whimper that you feel like a charity case!

AND NOT HIS WORST NIGHTMARE

Ask him to snuggle up
next to you in bed and
whisper, "I don't have
a headache tonight."

HOW TO BE THE WOMAN OF YOUR HUSBAND'S DREAMS

Crawl into bed in a high-neck, long-sleeve, full-length wool and corduroy nightgown.

123

AND NOT HIS WORST NIGHTMARE.

Invite him to an adventure flick and buy him a monster bucket of popcorn!

HOW TO BE THE WOMAN OF YOUR HUSBAND'S DREAMS

Take him to a three-hour, tear-jerking romance and cry through the entire movie.

AND NOT HIS WORST NIGHTMARE

Leave a note on
the coffee pot saying,
"You perk up my day!"

Drink your two cups
and turn off the pot
before he gets up.

AND NOT HIS WORST NIGHTMARE

Confess to him
that you're "captivated"
by his good looks.

HOW TO BE THE WOMAN OF YOUR HUSBAND'S DREAMS

Ask him if he had bad acne as a teenager.

AND NOT HIS WORST NIGHTMARE

Rub his neck and shoulders until he's putty in your hands.

HOW TO BE THE WOMAN OF YOUR HUSBAND'S DREAMS

When he is putty
in your hands,
ask for money!

131

AND NOT HIS WORST NIGHTMARE!

In the middle of the night when he tells you he is hot, turn up the air conditioner for him.

HOW TO BE THE WOMAN OF YOUR HUSBAND'S DREAMS

Tell him you're cold and turn up the heat.

133

AND NOT HIS WORST NIGHTMARE

Make yourself vulnerable! Tell him you never want to lose him.

HOW TO BE THE WOMAN OF YOUR HUSBAND'S DREAMS

Ask him how much insurance he has on himself should he suddenly die.

AND NOT HIS WORST NIGHTMARE

Tell him how smart he is.

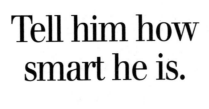

HOW TO BE THE WOMAN OF YOUR HUSBAND'S DREAMS

Point out you
make more money
than he does.

AND NOT HIS WORST NIGHTMARE

Remind him how much you appreciate "the little things" he does for you.

HOW TO BE THE WOMAN OF YOUR HUSBAND'S DREAMS

Exchange the ring
he gives you for a
bigger diamond.

AND NOT HIS WORST NIGHTMARE

When he gives you
a big ol' bear hug,
tell him he's your
"Teddy Bear."

HOW TO BE THE WOMAN OF YOUR HUSBAND'S DREAMS

Snap and growl
till he lets go.

AND NOT HIS WORST NIGHTMARE

141

Tell him he looks exceptional in a bathing suit.

Throw him a T-shirt.

AND NOT HIS WORST NIGHTMARE

At Christmas, chase
him around with
a sprig of Mistletoe.

HOW TO BE THE WOMAN OF YOUR HUSBAND'S DREAMS

Tell him he has the build to play Santa Claus.

AND NOT HIS WORST NIGHTMARE

Model for your kids how to respect their dad and speak to him with courtesy.

HOW TO BE THE WOMAN OF YOUR HUSBAND'S DREAMS

When the kids are belligerent and combative, yell at their dad to "be a man"!

AND NOT HIS WORST NIGHTMARE

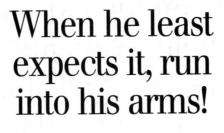

When he least
expects it, run
into his arms!

HOW TO BE THE WOMAN OF YOUR HUSBAND'S DREAMS

Run up his
credit cards.

AND NOT HIS WORST NIGHTMARE

When he's recuperating in the hospital from surgery, bring him his favorite magazines and CD's.

HOW TO BE THE WOMAN OF YOUR HUSBAND'S DREAMS

Remind him to eat his prunes.

AND NOT HIS WORST NIGHTMARE

151

Trust him implicitly.

HOW TO BE THE WOMAN OF YOUR HUSBAND'S DREAMS

Control him explicitly.

AND NOT HIS WORST NIGHTMARE

Apologize when you're wrong.

HOW TO BE THE WOMAN OF YOUR HUSBAND'S DREAMS

Never admit anything.

155

AND NOT HIS WORST NIGHTMARE

Additional copies of this book and
other titles are available
at your local bookstore.

157

TRADE LIFE BOOKS
P.O. Box 55325 • Tulsa, Oklahoma 74155